JOHNO and the Blind Chick

Sue-Ellen Lovett

A catalogue record for this book is available from the National Library of Australia

Important message from Johno

With my two beautiful brown eyes I will guide you

With my strong legs I will carry you with cadence

On my back you will ride with pride

With my heart I will love and look after you

Show me the way and I shall take you

Together we are as one

Together we shall soar.

1.

Well, standing in my paddock with my three paddock mates. Not long since breakfast. Just standing enjoying the sunshine. Then I hear the chain clinking on the gate. Someone is coming to get one of us. I wonder who that unlucky person is. He's going to get worked today.

Oh darn! It's me. "Johno," comes the word. "Come on Johno, let's go do some work, we have someone to meet you today."

Well as far as I knew, I had a few weeks off. I had a competition earlier on, a couple of months ago, and for all intents and purposes it was my time off. But apparently not so. The halter is put on and I am taken out of the paddock to the saddling up area. On my way, I went past many stables, horses in yards, horses on walking machines, horses being broken in. It is a very busy stable complex.

You have to realise the property I am on, there are 150 other horses. There are Show Jumpers. There are Eventers. There are even Racehorses preparing for their racing career. It is full on. I am just one of 150. I blend in pretty well, I stay out of trouble, I fly under the radar.

In the saddling up area, my coat is brushed, my hooves cleaned out, some fly spray applied with a soft brush, saddle pad and saddle put on and my bridle. There were four new people standing around while I was being tacked up. They were explaining a lot to a girl that was there. Then someone took her hand and guided her over to me. She felt me all over. She pats me. She talks to me. She seems okay. Bit of a sweetie I thought. But I didn't get much time to think about it. Nikki takes my reins and we were off over to the dressage arena.

Nikki mounts. The four new people follow along behind. I thought it was really cute. The man was holding the girl's hand all of the time. Really sweet hey. Must be really in love, I thought.

Nikki has a bit of a chat to these newcomers, and then we are off. Little bit of a walk around and a warmup. Bit of trotting, cantering, lateral work. You know, going sideways? Then Nikki dismounts. More chatter with these newcomers and next thing Nikki is handing my reins to the girl that was patting and talking to me before. Okay, looks like she's going to have a ride. Well, let's see what she is capable of doing.

Now, the few things I need to explain to you about me, I am 18.3 hands high. Which means there is no way I would fit through any standard front door. Very gentle and beautiful. But definitely tall.

The girl is escorted up to the mounting block. Everybody was giving her lots of instructions. Where things were and stuff like that. I didn't take much notice. But I thought it was a bit peculiar. So, she mounts and off we go for a walk around the arena. A couple of laps around the edge of the dressage arena in walk and we pop into a trot. All the time Nikki talking to the three newcomers left back there. No one is interacting with the girl who is riding me. They leave us alone.

So, while riding around it was really apparent that the girl was not doing much about turning in the corners. We were doing big 20-metre half circles at each end of the dressage arena, nothing that even resembled the corner. I thought this was a bit strange. But didn't give it much thought. Then a few other strange things started happening. The girl started doing some leg yields with me. Each time, she would count five strides to the right and then five strides back to the left out loud. Then we moved on forward. Wow she's pretty on the ball with all of this, counting strides and so forth. Then I was starting to add a few things up.

Everywhere she went she was guided. There were lots of explanations to her. Where things were, what was happening and it went on and on. Then it became apparent that she was relying on me a lot to navigate her around the arena. Apart from when she asked me to move away from her leg, where she would count her strides, I was virtually looking after her.

Oh, my heavens, then it dawned on me. Oh, my heavens, she is blind. Oh, what a responsibility I have. Now I need to be really conscious of what I'm doing and look after my lovely blind rider.

2.
A dream in the making

Well, the lovely girl dismounted and everyone said "what do you think? What do you think!" She said "Oh my heavens, he is just so beautiful and kind and gentle. He is every girl's dream!"

Then the girl had a chat with Nikki and talked about whether she was negotiable on the price. Nikki said no, and the girl said, we'll probably need to win lotto. She looked dejected and despondent. Tears running down her cheeks. It truly was an amazing ride. We had an amazing something that happened between us. It was like magic. Something that was meant to be.

Knowing that my price was way out of her price bracket, the girl said, thank you very much to Nikki, but also asked if she could come back on Monday for another ride. Nikki let all of the newcomers know that there was someone else coming to ride me on Monday. But said, she could come on Tuesday for a ride if she wanted to. With that, I made eye contact with the lovely girl's two beautiful hazel eyes (those two unseeing eyes). There were tears running down her cheeks. Thank you she said, and they left. It was really devastating knowing that we were never going to meet again, we really had something special happening.

3.
Who believes in magic?

Well, I have to tell the story now second hand. A story conveyed to me by the girl's mother-in-law Lee. The girl and the others travel back to Tone's, her husband's brother's place in Drummoyne. All the way back she was trying to think of a way she could afford to buy the beautiful horse that she had just ridden. She kept asking, her husband Matt, "can we talk about it now…" and he kept saying "no". She slowly turned her head towards the window, closing those unseeing eyes, tears run freely. All she could think about was the beautiful horse that she had just ridden and the magic that had transpired between her and Johno. It was just awesome. So much trust. So much beauty.

They get back to Tone's place and Matt's mum puts on a cuppa. Everybody sitting around the table. The girl asking Matt again "can we chat about it now?" "No!" he says. She is just devastated.

But those beautiful and unseeing eyes had no idea what was happening around her. Matt was doing sign language of thumbs up to his mum, while showing her his bank balance on his phone. Sitting there dejected, she just did not know what to do or how to cope with how she was feeling inside. Just totally devastated and heartbroken knowing she would never meet that beautiful Johno again.

Next thing Matt sat down with her and said "what did you think of the horse?" Her reply, "oh my heavens, he is what dreams are made of, he's what every young girl dreams of having, he is amazing and he looked after me so well. I even think he may have known I could not see." Matt continued, "would you like him? Would he suit you?" This seemed to be such a torment. Couldn't everybody else see how amazing he was, couldn't everybody else see how beautiful the relationship was right from the beginning. She replied, "oh my heavens, he is perfect, I could not think of a more beautiful horse to own, but that's not going to happen because I can't afford him, I have no way of paying for a horse like that. Way out of my league."

With that Matt said, "if you would like him, I will buy him for you." Those two beautiful unseeing eyes, tears streaming down "oh my heavens, thank you Matt, thank you from the bottom of my heart, what a wonderful gift. I am so grateful." Within ten minutes Matt was on the phone to Nikki getting her bank details and organising a vet check to be done on Johno. Everything went very quickly form there.

Next thing you know I'm at the vets having my heart checked, my lungs checked, my joints checked for flexibility and anything that may affect my movement. To my surprise, I passed with flying colours. I wonder what that means? Finally, back in the paddock with my mates, nothing seemed to change for a couple of days. I pulled a shoe and had another put back on. Watched the same old horses going around, being prepared for racing and schooled over jumps. Never a dull moment on the farm.

4.
A life changing experience

Well, unbeknownst to me, there had been a lot happening over the last five or six days. Out of the blue I was pulled out of the paddock again. Thought it was my time off. That girl came back, the girl I was sure could not see. But this time with only one sidekick, Janelle. She is being guided around by her friend Janelle, by holding onto her elbow. Janelle is giving her feedback with where they're going, what they're doing. Oh, my heavens, I was right. She is blind.

They had a white Ford Ranger Ute sitting outside my paddock with a saddle, bridles and other bits and pieces. They saddle me up, Janelle put together a new bridle for me and we go off into Nikki's dressage arena.

This time it was a bit better as the girl had her friend Janelle there giving her directions on where she was in the dressage arena and most importantly how far we were from the corners. This made it much easier for her to navigate me around the arena. We had a play for 45 minutes or so. It was a pleasant ride. Nothing ground breaking, but it was just another thing to consolidate out relationship. Something very special was brewing deep down in my heart. There was something very moving about this blind girl. She had a special confidence and belief in me.

The next day the girl's friend and professional saddle fitter, Jason from Wyong, came to do a saddle fitting on me to make sure her saddle fitted properly. Jason was a bit surprised by my size. "For a start 18.3 hands high is a little tall, I need a step ladder," Jason joked. So, he put the saddle on and it fitted perfectly. She made a deep sigh of relief, no need to buy a new saddle.

After making sure all the gear fitted me, the girls gave me a brush and had a chat. Then they took me down to my paddock and put me away again. I still had no idea what was happening. I thought I would never see her again. Having her around made me feel very special. It was like I was the only one, rather than one of 150. It's nice to feel that you are special, and the only one.

Well, I believe in miracles and magic. The next morning something pretty amazing happened. The two girls were back again. This time, they pulled up with a white horse float on the back. Janelle caught me, the girl was waiting at the float. She looked so excited, like a child opening presents on Christmas day. Janelle tried to put me on the float, but I wasn't quite sure whether I wanted to go on at first. I was a little bit hesitant. It took a little bit of persuading to get me on. After a while, I felt okay. It's all good I'll stay where I'm put, I thought. The girls latched the back of the horse float up and lifted the tail gate. We are off on a road trip.

Wow! All I could think about is, where am I going? This is a very long road trip. Am I going to a new home? We went over lots of big mountains out into the flat country. All I could see for miles was flat, dry plains. I tend to think they're in a pretty big drought out here. I hope they have grass where I am going.

5.
My new home

Wow! What a long trip over very big mountains, which I now know are the Blue Mountains. Down a very big hill called Mount Victoria, then we meandered past Windamere Dam through a beautiful little valley called Cudgegong Valley and then through Mudgee.

But it was very noticeable it was extremely dry. Looks like they are in a drought out here. Wow! Quite a few dead trees. No pasture in the paddock. Very few stock around. It was looking quite depressing.

But the Ranger and the horse float keep heading west, it is looking much dryer out here. The red soil looks parched like a moonscape. Cracks in the ground and still no stock around. Wow, not looking good!

We then drive through a major town; in fact, I think it is a city called Dubbo on reasonably good roads. But still heading west. Wow, where is this taking me? About twenty minutes out of Dubbo the car starts to slow and turns right up a drive. Well was I in for a tooth shaking experience. The corrugations in the road were terrible! I was shaken and stirred for a kilometre ride up the drive. Oh, my heavens the road was very rough.

Janelle and the girl get out of the Ranger and come to the back of the float to undo the tailgate to let me off. I still did not know what to expect. I could not see a horse in sight. Keeping in mind I came from a stable complex of 150 horses. Oh, my heavens, I am going to be so lonely.

Wow! It was so dry and parched here. Even the lucerne paddock looks sick. Looks like no irrigating had gone on for quite a while. The pasture paddocks were barren. One familiar thing, there was a dressage arena. Okay there might be other horses here says I.

Janelle quietly backs me off the horse float. I stand in absolute amazement. It is so flat out here. Where the heck am I? And still no other horses. I am so lonely already. But that lovely girl comes out and gives me a pat and a hug and a carrot. I am feeling very special and loved. But still lonely. Where are all the horses?

Janelle holds me while she takes off my floating boots and puts on a nice clean cotton rug. Janelle leads me through the pine trees and through the garden. Oh wow! There are other horses! There are two other horses! Can't wait to meet my neighbours!

Janelle takes me down and walks me around my paddock to familiarise me. She shows me where the big water trough is with lovely fresh water. I have a lovely stable with fresh pine shavings. It smells lovely. I also have a breeze way and a couple of paddocks that I can be rotated around so the food does not get sour. It looks okay for my digs.

Then she comes up again, this time she has this long white thing. I think they call it a white cane. Blind people use them. Wasn't sure about that thing! Not sure if I was gonna get smacked with it! She was waving it from side to side. I guess that is how she navigates, but I'm sure I will learn more as time goes on. With another hug and a big pat I am let go in my paddock. I run around for a while looking for the rest of those horses. Okay there are two here, but where are the rest of them?

I stopped long enough to meet Ben my next-door neighbour. He is a 22-year-old Warmblood Thoroughbred cross gelding. He used to be a dressage horse. And then next door to him is Sophie. She is a very pretty mare with long eyelashes. I think she fancies me and thinks I'm okay. But I am still looking for those other horses. This seems to be it. Two mates. Wow! But I am sure I will get used to it. Two mates are better than no mates.

Then later that afternoon I got a big surprise from the horses next door at the neighbour, Pete's place. They are trotters. Heavens, don't they move funny! They all came over and said hello and then trotted off down the paddock and left me to my other two friends Ben and Sophie.

When I stopped running around, I also realised I had a lovely paddock with a view. My paddock is on the Macquarie River. At the moment there is not a lot of water in it, but I bet it is pretty when there is water in it. And there is lots of birdlife, I even saw a couple of pelicans and a black swan.

6.
That blind girl

Standing in my paddock eating a lovely biscuit of lucerne hay, I quietly observed that blind girl who rode me down at Nicky's. There is something quite amazing happening between us already and I have only known her for such a very short time. There is this lovely feeling deep inside me. A feeling of familiarity, of love, of comfort and I feel like I need to look after her.

Wherever she goes she has that white cane thing in front of her waving it from right to left and back again. I definitely think it is an aid to help her navigate her way around the property and not run into trees or gardens.

She is very conscious of not leaving the white cane outside when she comes into my paddock, so she does not upset me or frighten me. I think she is worried about hitting my legs with a white cane. But I'm sure I will get used to it in time. It is just weird, but I suppose it is better than running into a tree or tripping over a garden bed.

I am given a day to settle in. Lots of visits from the lovely blind girl. Each time she comes down she calls my name, "Johno" and brings a carrot for me. She is pretty cool! Love the carrot idea and also don't mind the pat and brush. This is all really lovely.

You know this is all turning out a little bit of alright. Instead of being one of 150, I am the only one. The only one she feeds, the only one she brushes, the only one in her heart. This is too cool. I think I have found my forever home.

Each morning and each evening I am brought a lovely feed of pellets and a lovely big biscuit of hay. Lucerne hay, apparently her husband Matthew makes lucerne hay, and I must say it is beautiful. Probably my favourite part of breakfast and dinner is my lucerne hay.

Early the next morning the blind girl is down to feed me. It is a Monday and she is telling me about a friend of hers Karen, who is keen to come out and help her with me and get to know me. I can't wait to meet Karen, she sounds lovely.

Well didn't have to wait long. At about 8.30 in the morning, Karen and the blind girl come down through the garden, Karen guiding her. Karen stops at the gate and picks up my halter and they both come down through my gate into my paddock. I walk up to meet them, the blind girl might have a carrot.

I think this journey with the blind girl is going to be interesting. Not sure how things are going to play out, but I am sure willing to learn and make life easier for her. I also noticed on her veranda she had a black dog. That was her guide dog Amani who used to guide her around.

Amani did not get used at all on the farm, she only used Amani when she went to town and when she would travel away to do speaking engagements. Amani must be very clever because Amani takes the blind girl on the plane as well. Wow, how cool!

The blind girl places the halter on me and Karen leads me and the blind girl back up to the tack shed. I have a good look around the garden. Could do with a bit of a water, but there's not enough water in the river to irrigate the garden. I think the water in my water trough is from a bore, you know the underground river water. The water is really lovely and clean and clear.

We get up to the tack shed and my lessons start. One of the things that Karen and the blind girl are instilling in me is that I am responsible for where I keep my four feet. And when I am put at the tack shed, I am expected to stand there. At first Karen held me and they will give me moments when she would drop the lead and the expectation was for me not to move. This I thought was rather interesting, as when I lived down over the mountains with all those other horses I was tied up, so this is an interesting process. A process in teaching and letting me be responsible for what I do and how I react. I tend to think this is a bit of okay and for me to be responsible is a big thing, because normally everyone takes the responsibility from me.

Karen and the blind girl give me a good brush, clean my hooves out, put some oil on my hooves and then take me for a walk to familiarise me with the area. We walk out through the pine trees out into the garden over towards the dressage arena. There is also a round yard there. I'm sure I will spend some time in there learning different things.

We walked out to the dressage arena, Karen leading me and guiding the girl. We walked around the dressage arena a few times familiarising me with the arena. But the biggest thing was, oh my heavens it is so flat! Out here there are no hills, it is also very dry and dusty. They are really in the middle of a big-time drought. Everything is so brown and dead. Feeling hopeful that it rains soon.

The next day we did more of the same, more familiarisation. This time I had my saddle on and Karen lined me up with the mounting block for the blind girl to mount. Now remember when she rode me before it took me a little while to realise that she could not see, so now I have to be more responsible. I must be her eyes. I have to have her back and look after her and guide her around the arena safely.

Not sure what we are going to do about the corners in the dressage arena because the dressage arena surround is just a little plastic thing about 18 inches high. Barely a twig for me to walk out over the edge of. I think I am meant to stay inside, but will see how things play out. As we are riding around Karen calls out to the blind girl when she is coming up to the corner to turn. She doesn't ride me deep into the corners, she just does half circles around the corner so I'm not in a position to walk out over the edge of the arena.

After a couple of days riding the blind girl gets the confidence to put me into a trot, and again we're not going into the corners, we are just doing big 20 metre half circles. A dressage arena is 20 metres by 60 metres. On the short side, the 20 metre side, she does 20 metre half circles up there, not going into the corner and always pushing me off her inside leg into the outside rein, so I stay on the track. This is a bit cool.

The other thing I learned about the blind girl is the fact that she usually only rides of a morning. This is because she generally starts off on the right-hand rein and the sun is on the left side of her face which is on the East. This gives her what is called orientation and gives her an idea of where she is in the arena. This helps a little bit I think, maybe so she doesn't get lost so much, if she has an idea of what direction she is going in. I am sure an overcast day would not be easy when you can't see.

Well this living with a blind girl is turning out to be quite interesting. Lots more responsibility for me when being ridden but enjoying the challenge and enjoying looking after my new best friend.

My training in the saddle and on the ground continues. I am continually stepping up to the mark and taking on more responsibility. But the next challenge is amazing. Wow! Am I so proud of what I am learning to do? It is so very cool that we do this together and eventually without Karen's help.

The blind girl and I are becoming best friends. So, I give her a nick name. My Blind chick! She is a bit of a spunky chick! The journey of Johno and the blind chickie babe begins.

7.
Johno the guide horse

Well things were progressing along nicely. Each morning Monday to Friday Karen arrives out at the farm and will bring The Blind Chick down to catch me.

I heard them discussing one day on the walk down about how her guide dog worked. That it would guide her from point A to point B and she thought there would be no reason whatsoever why I could not do this. So, the girls put in process a plan to teach me to be a guide horse. They first started with me guiding The Blind Chick up from the horse paddock to the tack shed.

Each time I did this I was rewarded with a piece of carrot. But this reward system of a piece of carrot distracted me from doing anything else afterwards, as I wanted to look in all their pockets to check they did not have any more treats for me. So, guess what, the carrots were soon taken away as my reward and it was just lots of praise and cuddles and the odd carrot when I had done something super-dooper special.

So, I was picking up this guide horse gig really quickly. I was becoming exceptionally good at bringing The Blind Chick up to the tack shed and standing while Karen and the chickie babe tacked me up and put my work boots on. Then Karen started with teaching me to guide The Blind Chick out to the dressage arena. Now this is quite a long way through the garden and lots of lovely green grass, so it was up to me to be very strong and diligent and do the right thing and not stop and eat the grass. This was a wee problem sometimes.

Firstly, they started with me guiding The Blind Chick out to the dressage arena. With my blind chick walking at my shoulder, her hand on my neck and the rein in her left hand I would walk out with Karen in front of us I would follow Karen. As things progressed Karen walked to the side to make sure everything was okay and The Blind Chick was safe.

Well things progressed really quickly. Within two or three weeks I had this being a guide horse mastered. I could bring The Blind Chick up from my paddock through the gate up to the tack shed. Okay this sounds a bit monotonous, but it is all part of the training. They would then give me a brush, clean my feet out and put my work boots on. Then they would saddle me up and put my bridle on, The Blind Chick would come and stand at my left shoulder and do a couple of clicks with her tongue and I would then guide her out to the dressage arena. As time went on Karen just walked behind us, as she was not needed to give me any direction or anything. It was pretty cool. I felt very proud of myself being able to look after my Blind Chick. The next thing was to teach me to line up at the mounting block so she could get on me easily.

This I took to very quickly. I realised that The Blind Chick could not get on me from the ground, she definitely needed the mounting block, as I am so tall. So, after two or three adjustments and a week's training I had that one under my belt as well. This was pretty cool. I was making lots of decisions and I was helping out big time. I had to look after my Blind Chick, and I was doing a great job

So, once I lined up at the mounting block she would walk up the three little steps and stand on the top step and get on my back. We would stand and do some flexing and softening exercises. I would have to bring my head round and touch her toe on the left side then bring my head round and touch her toe on the right side. We did this for about five minutes getting me nice and soft and supple, then we would go off into the arena at a walk and warmup.

Each day varied when we rode. Some days it would be just a lovely long walk for 45 minutes, other days we will do lots of trot work and canter work and transitions. Always working on my softness and always working on me being supple, so lots of lateral work. Now this means getting me to go sideways and move off her leg. This is either called leg yielding or a half pass. I'm even getting good at this dressage lingo.

One of the big things The Blind Chick and Karen were working on with me was also keeping me calm and happy, trying to introduce no tension. This meant the rhythm and regularity did not change and it was easier for The Blind Chick to stay orientated. Eventually she would do even more counting strides, like she did the first time she rode me.

So, after we worked in the dressage arena each day The Blind Chick would ask me to halt down the end of the arena near the letter A and she would dismount. Then it was up to me, Johno the guide horse. How cool is this to lead my blind chickie babe out of the dressage arena, around the round yard, across the gardens, through the pine trees, and back to the tack shed to be unsaddled, given a bath, a carrot and a clean rug.

All the time that I'm doing this guiding she is telling me what a good boy I am and what a good job I am doing. This is very cool. What a special job I have since I moved here. I have lots of responsibility, to look after my blind chick on the ground and in the saddle. I love this job. It is awesome and we are best mates.

How much have things changed? I have gone from being one of 150 horses and not a high-profile horse. I was just one of the crew. Did my dressage, got ridden, gave lessons and that was me in a nutshell. Now I have the love and care of one person. I am her only horse, she feeds me, she brushes me, she comes down and just sits and talks to me. I sit and listen to her talking and telling stories about her book. We have a lovely bond that is growing stronger and stronger each day.How lucky am I that this lovely blind girl with the unseeing hazel eyes came to visit me and thought she would like to take me home. How amazing is this and the fact that her wonderful husband Matthew could see something special in our relationship on our first ride. Totally so happy and grateful and blessed. She is no longer a strange blind rider, she is my Blind Chick.

8.

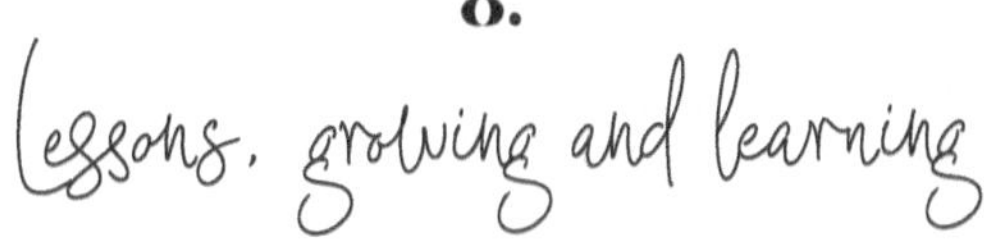

Things are going nicely with The Blind Chick and I. There is a weekend when Karen isn't able to be with us, so Matthew comes out to help us and sometimes gives us lessons. Sometimes this is really interesting and sometimes there are quite a few arguments. But the eyes on the ground that are able to see what we were doing are so beneficial. Matthew's lessons are terrific and a few little problems that The Blind Chick had, like her moving her right hand instead of keeping it nice and still are addressed, also making sure she is sitting tall with those heels down.

This went on for quite a few weekends with Matthew giving us lessons and then The Blind Chick was talking to Karen and thought she needed to get some help from a proper coach. She had previously had lessons with a lovely lady called Cathy from Millthorpe, who is a great mate and used to be a fellow competitor. So, she got in contact with Cathy and asked if she and Trevor would come over and give us some lessons.

In normal situations you would go to your coach and take your horse but because my rider is blind we need to be very conscious of the fact that I need to be within an enclosed area. If it is a flat area with just tiny little poles I would walk or trot right out and The Blind

Chick would not know where she is. So, it was important to train in her own environment. She was most grateful when Cathy said she and Trevor would come over and give her lessons for a couple of days. It was terrific.

She also organised for her good friend Prue to come and take some photos of us working. Prue is a professional photographer and takes beautiful photos. A bit quirky, don't you think, that The Blind Chick wanted photos. But she wanted them to share with all her friends on Facebook. So, Prue came down and took some beautiful photos. Her mother-in-law, Lee, also took some beaut photos so she had a lovely collection very early on of us working together.

Cathy worked on building up The Blind Chick's confidence and to ride me forward. In the beginning I think she may have been a little bit of a passenger, overwhelmed by the whole deal of a new horse and the fact that she never knows where she is in the arena. Must be so very daunting.

So, Cathy made us focus on going a little more forward and a little more uphill. We also did lots of transitions. This means transitions up from walk to trot and trot to canter and transitions down from canter to trot and trot to walk. You can also have transitions within the one gait, so you can collect the canter, or you can push the canter out or you can collect the trot and then push the trot out and collect again. These are wonderful exercises for getting me engaged and working from behind like I should be. Doing the lessons were awesome, we both learnt so much. Cathy you're such a super-dooper coach!

During the lesson I could feel The Blind Chick's confidence growing. It was a wonderful feeling! She was starting to own the ride, she was riding me more forward, confidently doing half halts, asking me to slow and then canter on again. It was so nice to feel this confidence building and our partnership getting stronger each stride.

After Cath's lesson The Blind Chick had lots of homework to work on. So, each day we rode she would go through all of the things Cath had taught us from our lesson the weeks before, and slowly but surely, apart from the confidence growing, our bond and our working together got stronger. What a cool feeling. We were starting to become as one.

It was really difficult with us not being able to ride anywhere there wasn't an enclosed area. This limited her ability to go somewhere and train. So once again Cath and Trevor came over and we had more lessons, but this was not a sustainable situation.

The Blind Chick then did some homework and got onto a beautiful young lady called Melanie who is down at Cessnock. Melanie had a lovely arena with big wooden fence sides, this would be just ideal for us to train and for my blind chickie babe to be safe.

So, The Blind Chick organised for us to go down to Cessnock for lessons with Melanie. Karen would drive us down and we would go for two or three days, just depending if Melanie could fit us in. We had a terrific time down there and we learnt so much.

Melanie worked a lot on The Blind Chick's posture and my straightness on the left rein. I am not as straight on the left rein, so it was important to keep my neck quite straight when I am on the left rein and then when you're on the right rein a little bit of softness and flexion to the right. It was so cool. It made such a difference to when we were doing diagonals and keeping me straight. All these things are just so very important when you are getting ready to do a dressage test, and that is our goal.

So, every three or four weeks Karen, The Blind Chick and I would pack up the float and head down to Melanie's at Cessnock for lessons. Each time we went down for lessons The Blind Chick would get Melanie to ride me, to feel if she had been doing her homework and had me travelling nicely. Melanie was always complimentary about us being up to date on our homework, but we were still working on the straightness and The Blind Chick was still working on that right hand. Melanie jokes that someone needs to come and connect her elbow to her hip to help her keep a steady hand. Just a little too busy with that right hand. But it is improving. She hooks her thumb in the monkey grip on the right-hand side. The monkey grip is a little strap that goes across the top of the saddle and helps her keep her hands more still. This is much nicer for me as my mouth is not being touched or jerked on if you have steady hands.

9.
Surgery

While riding down at Melanie's it became quite apparent, in fact Melanie pointed it out to The Blind Chick, that she needed a stronger core and stronger leg muscles and that she needed to probably go to the gym and rectify this situation. I thought this was rather funny, but the blind chickie babe was not that impressed. So, she organised to go to the gym to work on her core and her leg muscles.

She went to the gym a couple of times and I'm sure it was making a difference and then one morning after riding she was lying on the floor doing leg lifts and something weird was flashing in her right eye. Keeping in mind she has no sight, just grey fog. But something was flashing, and her eye was starting to do a lot of aching. So, she put up with this for a while and thought she better go to the optometrist to see what was wrong.

So, The Blind Chick rang the optometrist and got an appointment with Tony. The optometrist put drops in her eyes to dilate the pupils and Tony had a bit of a look in her eyes. It became quite apparent there was not such good things happening in the back of her eyes, particularly the right eye. Her lens and lens capsule had collapsed and was sitting on the back of the retina. This was not good, and this is what was causing all the pain. Tony suggested that The Blind Chick not ride. But good luck with that one. She cut the riding back a bit, but then she had to go to the ophthalmologist.

The ophthalmologist had a look at her eye, and he said you need surgery and you need it very soon otherwise, I know you are blind but it could cause more damage in your eye and more pain. This is not a good thing, so The Blind Chick was booked in for surgery and this meant no riding. Oh, my heavens what's going to happen to our work routine and who's gonna look after me? I was getting very worried.

The Blind Chick had a big chat with Melanie and asked if I could go down and stay at her place and if Melanie could train me while she had her eye surgery and while she was recuperating. Her eye surgeon said it would be at least six weeks before she could even be contemplating sitting on a horse, possibly eight weeks.

So, Karen and The Blind Chick take me down to Melanie's with all my feed, my horse rugs, my additives, and I thought I was being deserted and left. I was so lonely! Melanie was very busy and had lots of other horses to work as well as me, and I went back to being just one of the mob. I was devastated. I missed her, I missed my blind chick that I used to look after. I thought she wasn't coming back.

So, my blind chick goes into surgery, I organised to have some flowers and a lovely little teddy that she can cuddle sent to her in hospital. Then just waited and waited and waited and still my blind chick and Karen had not returned. One week went past. Two weeks went past. Three weeks went past. Still no visits. She's not coming back; she's not coming to get me. But little did I know she was coming the week after.

Well, wow! What a wonderful surprise, early one morning Melanie was working in the dressage arena and the white Ford Ranger pulled up, and out of the car gets Karen and The Blind Chick. WOOHOO! My day is made. My beautiful blind chick is back, and she's gonna come and take me home. I know she is I, know she is. We are going to go home.

But that was not to be, unbeknownst to me I was staying for a few more weeks as The Blind Chick was not allowed to ride or be near me too much because it was so important for her not to get an infection in her eye. She gave me a couple of cuddles and lots of carrots and she promised she would be back soon. The feeling of devastation when she leaves is horrible. I feel so alone.

Summer training with Melanie continues five days a week and I'm getting very fit and looking terrific. But it is so lonely without my blind chick. I have other mates in paddocks beside me, but it's not the same as having your best friend there to look after you and love you.

About seven weeks after The Blind Chick had surgery she turns up with Karen and has a chat to Melanie. She made the decision there and then to take me home. I was so happy! I had my ride with Melanie that morning and then Karen and The Blind Chick put me on the float, and we were going home. I was so excited to be back with my beautiful blind chick. Could not wait until I got back in my paddock at home, and I would be number one again.

I had a great drive home. Karen took me off the float and took me down to my paddock. I ran around for a while and went and said hello to my mate Ben and then down to Sophie and said g'day I'm back guys! I'm back! I am so happy. So, that afternoon she feeds me and gives me a lovely big biscuit of lucerne hay. I am home. I am happy, and I am content.

When The Blind Chick was recovering, Karen had done lots of work with me when she would visit me down at Melanie's. Desensitising me and getting me used to the white cane. So now when she came down she used the white cane to navigate to the stable to feed me and then to go and get my hay. But she was not riding me. What's wrong? Why am I not being ridden? I don't understand why we aren't going out and playing in the dressage arena. I miss our rides.

Well again another one of those things unbeknownst to me The Blind Chick had been back to her ophthalmologist and he had given her the worst news you could ever give this beautiful blind chick. He told her she was never to ride again. She was devastated. She came home and cried and cried and cried and could not make sense of it. The surgeon was worried that if she rode and had a jar, that it would undo all of the work he had done on fixing her eye. Plus, her left eye was going to collapse very soon, and she would need more surgery. Oh, my heavens, what are we going to do?

The Blind Chick rang her husband Matthew absolutely distraught, in tears. Inconsolable tears. The surgeon told her she was never to ride again. She sobbed into the phone, "what will I do? What will I do? All I live for is to ride." She cried, and "I have my beautiful Johno in the paddock. What will I do? I can't not ride," she sobbed.

Matthew, in his usual cool way explained to The Blind Chick "what else can go wrong, you are already totally blind, so what have you got to lose?" So, with that the sobbing slowly quietened and she gave it some thought. She said to Matthew, "you are right you know, I have nothing to lose, I am already totally blind, I'm starting riding again tomorrow." Wow, these are beautiful words to my ears. I was so excited to know that my beautiful blind chick was going to be back in the saddle, and we would be continuing on our amazing journey together. Having fun playing, fulfilling our goals and dreams.

10.
Back on track again

The first few days back we did quite a bit of work in the round yard, Karen teaching me liberty work. I was working without a halter to the commands of Karen. Pretty cool. You have to be on the ball, and I have to have my attention on what Karen is teaching me, otherwise I go wayward when I should be listening. So being focused is very important when you do liberty work.

So, we had been working in the round yard for two or three days now and still The Blind Chick was not riding. I was a bit worried about this. I was concerned that she was worried about hurting her eye and what the surgeon had said, or whether she had lost some of her confidence because it had been nearly two months since she had been riding. Keeping in mind she had not had me for that long before she had her eye surgery. So, it could've been a little bit of both.

Under Karen's supervision and encouragement, The Blind Chick gets back into the saddle and we get back into the arena. But it becomes pretty obvious very quickly that The Blind Chick is struggling a little with confidence. The Blind Chick decided that we needed to go somewhere to beat the heat and with someone she believed in. We were getting weeks on end of up to 45°C. This was not good for man or beast riding.

The Blind Chick rang her good friend Robyn Smith, who lives in Scone to see if she could fit her in for some lessons. Robyn has a lovely indoor arena and a wonderful complex where I would be quite comfortable with training in the heat.

So, it was organised. Another road trip. Karen, The Blind Chick and I were off to Scone to have lessons with Robyn. We left extremely early as travelling during the middle of the day in this heat is a killer for horses, and they did not want me to get dehydrated. So early trip it was. We arrived at Robyn's at about eleven in the morning. Nearly forgot to mention the drive into Robyn's. Once we left the main road, we went onto a dirt road. Oh, my heavens, talk about shaken not stirred. The road was so corrugated and bumpy. I had to check if my teeth were still in there when we pulled up. After that ordeal, I was put in the paddock for a bit of a rest. Later in the day the girls came back and The Blind Chick rode me.

Robyn helped The Blind Chick overcome her lack of confidence very quickly. Robyn is very passionate and dedicated, and just inch by inch she helped The Blind Chick ride through her stress.

After The Blind Chick's lesson, Karen gave me a good bath and carrot. Robyn gave The Blind Chick a good talking to about the fact that she needed to get a stronger core and more strength in her legs. So, I tend to think we have heard this before. But it was good to hear someone giving her a bit of a rev up.

Robyn proceeded to show The Blind Chick a few exercises. Oh, my heavens, The Blind Chick couldn't even entertain trying to do them. Robyn is an absolute ball of muscle, and energy, and has such strength in her core and her leg muscles. Wow! The Blind Chick was very envious. But it also took a lot of dedication for Robyn to have such a strong core and muscles, as she works out at the gym very, very regularly.

So, The Blind Chick chatted with Robyn about going to the gym. Back home I still don't think this has happened. In fact, I probably don't think it will happen. I know she is eating healthy, and hoping that her core muscles will build up just with riding. We shall see.

The next two days, The Blind Chick and I had a couple of great lessons. It was wonderful for building The Blind Chick's confidence, having Robyn coaching her. They are great mates and The Blind Chick has great faith in Robyn. This helps a lot when you are not feeling so confident.

Robyn had us doing some lovely flying changes across the diagonal and some very nice canter pirouette exercises. I do mighty fine canter pirouettes, even if I do say so myself. It was lots of fun, and we had a great time learning. But most of all, it was an exercise in building up The Blind Chick's confidence.

Oh, I must tell you of something else that happened while at Scone. It was really lovely. We stayed with Karen's mother and father-in-law, Charlie and Pam. As you do when you go to stay with someone, you generally take a bottle of wine or flowers or something. Karen did the introductions between The Blind Chick, Pam and Charlie and they invited them in.

Well this is a lesson on how to win friends and influence people. Karen was guiding The Blind Chick down the hall at Charlie and Pam's, and The Blind Chick had her backpack on her back. As she went past a table in the hallway she knocked off a beautiful vase and flowers. Oh, my heavens! Apparently, The Blind Chick was so embarrassed. Karen was sharing the story with me afterwards. I tend to think The Blind Chick felt really bad about breaking the vase and flowers. Oopsie!

After our early lesson with Robyn on the Wednesday, I had a bath and we packed up and headed back to Dubbo. We left early again to beat the heat. It is generally about a four and a half to five hour trip with the horse float on. It wasn't a bad run and the heat wasn't too bad. Karen brought The Blind Chick a thermometer to put in the float. It sends the temperature reading to a device in the car. Karen kept a very close eye on the temperature for me in the back of the float. But all was good.

We travelled with both barn doors opened in the back and all windows open, so great circulation of wind. Mind you, it being hot wind. But the wind was circulating. We all arrived home safe and sound. I was put back in my paddock and straight away, head down eating the lovely grass. Thank you, Robyn for the great lessons.

Building on what we have

It was time for The Blind Chick to work out what she had and what she wanted. I tend to think she had quite a bit of time to think over the two months of not riding on how she would like to move forward with our relationship and our training. More so our training, because I think our relationship was strong and is getting stronger every day. But the training worried her. I am very obliging and want so much to help and please. I am an ask, don't tell horse. But I want so bad to do it right and keep my beautiful blind chick happy.

I know in the past she has had many horses, and her last horse Desiderata she trained up to Grand Prix. Which is a massive achievement, even when you can see.

Four years prior she had an amazing gentleman and his wonderful family the Snow family come into her life and sponsor her and Desiderata. The Snow Foundation and Willinga Park helped make her dreams come true. The amazing Terry and family paid for her training, going to competitions, the accommodation of her living markers, which there were eight of. It was a major production to get The Blind Chick and her horse to a competition and into the arena. This is not a matter of a one-man band, and a blind chick, and a journey. It is a team of amazing people that are dedicated and help The Blind Chick make her dreams come true. It is truly remarkable.

Dressage training and dedication are not new to The Blind Chick, but she has been thinking that she would like to do it differently with me, possibly along a different path. Still wanting to do the dressage and compete and do demonstrations, which she loves. But the training side of things, she would like to approach it differently.

So firstly, Karen introduces the liberty work and that is going really well, and I am responding beautifully to it. I love the liberty work; it is excellent and it is really cool. You have to be focused and listen and watch what Karen is letting you know because very rarely does she speak. It is all done with commands with the whip. When Karen puts the whip up you go, when the whip comes down you slow and whip on the ground you stop. Pretty clear and concise instructions, but you have to pay attention. I am doing really well with my liberty work. Obviously, the liberty work is not suitable for The Blind Chick to be doing as I have no halter or lunge lead on. I am just free in the round yard and I often play and muck around, so this would be quite dangerous to somebody who can't see. But Karen manages the liberty work beautifully and I have learnt so much with her.

So, the next thing The Blind Chick would like to do is in-hand work which Karen has started on, and we are going for coaching with José. I will let you know how that goes. I know she is very excited about doing the in-hand work. She is also keen to do some natural dressage training, which is airing more on asking, not telling and rewarding lots more than you usually would do in traditional dressage training.

With the in-hand work, Karen has been working on getting me to lift my hooves one at a time and then working on lifting my back hooves. This is the start to the movement called piaffe, which is one of the hardest movements in dressage. It is pretty cool I have got the gist of things, and I know she is going to chat to Karen about maybe being on me bareback when Karen does the next lot of exercises. This may make a big difference as The Blind Chick can control the front end with the bridle and Karen can keep the energy in the backend getting the legs to move up and down. It will be interesting to see how this plays out.

We have done a couple of sessions with a lot of desensitisation. When The Blind Chick rides at the moment with her living markers, they all wear white coats so they can be picked out from the rest of the people at the dressage competition. They are the only ones that are allowed to stand close to the dressage arena, right beside the letter and they will call the letters as she and I will be riding around the arena. So, if she is heading towards H the person standing at H will be going "H, H, H, H," and then she rides on to the next letter which will be "E, E, E, E."

When you think about it, there will be a lot happening. The Blind Chick will have to know the dressage test. She will have to have been counting her strides, and know where she is in the arena for her preparation for the movements, and then with the living markers giving her direction and keeping her straight when she does a diagonal or rides down the centre line. This is imperative to get good scores in a dressage test, so lots to do and lots to think about.

But getting back to the whitecoats, The Blind Chick has been wearing a white coat around the outside of the round yard while

Karen is doing liberty work with me, so I get used to the people in white coats. She is also kicking a drum around and using her white cane to make quite a lot of noise. Sometimes this can be really distracting, but it is definitely desensitising.

The latest thing my beautiful blind chick has brought into the mix has been riding bareback. She has got a loan of a bareback pad off a beautiful friend Beck and has been riding me bareback. Well this is a hoot, seeing as she doesn't have the best balance at the best of times. She often has a wobbly boot on when she is walking because she can't see, she cannot see the horizon, so she has nothing to gauge what is straight. So, her riding bareback has been a very interesting experience. It is also very good for her balance so this should improve. It is also very good for her core muscles so maybe she may not need to go to the gym, who knows.

So, the first day in the bareback pad there was just lots of walking around quietly in the round yard, a little bit of trotting. But she lost her balance a little bit and came back to a walk and then tried to trot again. But each time getting a little bit more confident and it was important for me to stay nice and slow and soft through the back, so she had a good ride.

After her first ride bareback, she was stoked, and she was also hooked on riding bareback. She just wants things to go back to like it was when she was a child. The joy of riding bareback. Okay she won't be cantering up in the hills and riding through rivers like she did when she was a child. But she can have that joy of being as one riding bareback in the round yard and hopefully we will progress to the dressage arena very soon.

The Blind Chick's second ride bareback was much better. She was much more relaxed and had long legs just dangling and relaxing. We did some walk; we did a little bit of trot and then guess what she popped me into the canter. Oh, my heavens she was elated. I have a very big bold canter, but it is very soft, and quiet, and slow. It was magic. "This is what dreams are made of," said The Blind Chick. She was so chuffed and so happy. We did lots of transitions, she worked on her position, sitting nice and tall, and worked on trying to keep that right hand still as it jiggles around sometimes.

She did a couple of exercises walking across the round yard and turning and doing a walk pirouette and then walking the other way. I do pretty fine walk pirouettes, even if I do say so myself. But it was pretty cool the sensation for my blind chick riding bareback and feeling this under her, it was lovely. Then back into the canter and we were doing canter, walk, canter transitions. This was very cool, and I was very engaged and very responsive.

The blind chickie babe then must've had a bolt of confidence hit her, because then she brought me in near the middle of the round yard and asked me to shorten my stride and put me into a canter pirouette, which is quite a difficult movement when you can see and when you have a saddle on, let alone being blind and in a bareback pad. Well I did quite a fancy tight canter pirouette, this put her a little off balance, but it was all okay. She was giggling and had so much fun. She said to Karen, "I have to try that the other way." So, we changed rein and had a go the other way. The biggest problem was The Blind Chick's balance, and because the canter pirouette was nice and tight, she lost her balance a little bit. But it did not matter, she was sitting nice and straight and had the bareback pad on. Possibly if she did not have the bareback pad on she may have slid right off. But it was well done, and well recovered and both canter pirouettes were quite nice. Probably a little tidier when she has the saddle on, but that's okay. We are playing and enjoying ourselves and learning.

At the moment we are hopefully at the end of the drought and we having some lovely rain and also thunderstorms go through. This is interfering a little with our training, but it is all good. The rain is beautiful. The grass is growing in my paddock, and so are the weeds.

Really looking forward to our next bareback ride. I tend to think The Blind Chick is getting more confident and more game each ride. Heaven knows what she will try next, but I am up for it. It is such cool fun. It is so nice to be playing and enjoying and I am having fun. It is so cool.

After we have finished our work we come in to the tack shed, I am unsaddled and then we go out into the yard and go looking for some lush grass for me to have a pick on. It is just all so very relaxing and lovely. Karen and The Blind Chick stand and chat, I eat and have lots of cuddles and pats and brushes. I am feeling the love. I am so happy to be in the environment I am in and be the love of the life of The Blind Chick.

12.
Dressage Arena Marker Announcer (DAMA)

Well about four years ago The Blind Chick approached a very clever young man called Andrew Burfitt about getting a solar fan for her horse's stable. This conversation progressed from one thing to another. Next thing she had suggested, could he make a system to call the letters around the dressage arena?

With this question Andrew did not bat an eyelid. He was confident he could create and make a system to call the letters around the dressage arena. The Blind Chick was very excited about this, as this would make things much easier for her to train at home and also not to have to take eight people as living markers to call her dressage test. So, things progress from there. What an exciting thought. How much easier would things be.

So, Andrew set about designing a gadget that would call the letters around the dressage arena as you were coming to them. Someone sits at the end of the arena with the control panel and pushes the "C" and "C" again and "C" again, and this gives The Blind Chick direction where to ride. The person holding the control panel pushes each letter multiple times. As she rides the speaker is calling the letter which gives her the direction to ride to. It is interesting how many people think it would work putting earphones into her ears and telling her where to go but think about it. That does not give you direction when it is in your head. You need to have the noise coming from where you need to go, so this idea was going to work really well.

Mind you The Blind Chick and I will be using the living markers for a little while at competitions when we get out and about as they give her quite a lot of confidence. Having the eight people around the arena calling the letters is rather spectacular to watch and quite moving. These beautiful living markers give the blind girl the ability to ride a dressage test. How very cool is that.

A few weeks ago, there was a big lot of boxes arrive. The Blind Chick and Karen unpack the boxes. There were twelve receiver boxes, twelve speakers, chargers and the control panel. They set about organising it in bags inside a great big container so they can wheel it around from A to B and keep it nice and secure and weatherproof. They then set about desensitising me with the audio system. They then took a couple of the arena markers out to the round yard and placed them around the round yard and The Blind Chick was in charge of the control panel.

So, every now and again I would hear "K, K, K, K," and then she would start pushing the other arena marker sound which was "B, B, B, B," as I was coming around. She was also wearing one of the white coats that the living markers use when they are calling the letters and wondering around the round yard desensitising me. This is just so I was in the loop of what was happening and there were no surprises, because the last thing I need is a fright and shy and give the blind chickie babe a big scare. So, it is a really good idea to put the ground work in first with the desensitisation which is working a treat.

All of this work is paying off big time. We are just waiting for the weather to clear and the dressage arena to dry out, as it is flooded at the moment, so we can have a play with the full dressage arena marker announcers. It should be cool fun. I know she is really looking forward to trialling it and also getting to practice doing a centreline or a straight diagonal. This should be wonderful. What a great innovation. Thank you so much Andrew.

13.
The vet

Well it was a lovely Saturday morning, still very much in the grips of the drought. Everything was very dry and bare, and I wasn't feeling the best. Had what you would call a bit of a tummy ache happening which was making me feel very uncomfortable. I stood around for a while and then I started pawing the ground. My tummy was hurting, and then I pawed at the ground some more and I had a roll and then pawed the ground some more. I didn't quite know what was wrong, but I knew something wasn't right.

Well, I must say there is nothing at all wrong with The Blind Chicks hearing because after the second time I had rolled and done some more pawing she was out the front door listening. She called Matthew and she flew round the side of the house, got her white cane, put her boots on and was in my paddock in a milli second. She had the halter on me and was walking me, I still had my tummy ache. I wanted to roll. I wanted to paw at the ground and kick at my tummy. I had a really bad tummy ache. It was horrible.

She walked me for about half an hour, but my tummy ache was not getting better. If anything, I was more uncomfortable. So, she called out to Matthew her husband who comes and takes over leading me around the paddock to try and get rid of my tummy ache. The Blind

Chick goes and rings the vet with an urgent call. "Johno has colic," she is really scared. If a big horse like myself goes down and keeps rolling they can twist their bowel and this can be really catastrophic and mean surgery, so it is important that she kept me moving and waited for the vet to come. She was quite panicked and quite worried.

But the tummy ache persisted. It was a Saturday afternoon and this meant The Blind Chick was calling the vet out after hours. This was not a problem to her, it was just a matter of the vet getting there as soon as possible as my tummy ache was getting much worse as time went on. The vet arrived and she gave me a sedative and a painkiller to take away my tummy ache. She then put a hose down my nose and a tube down into my tummy. She then mixed up a concoction of oil and psyllium husks and pumped this down the tube into my tummy. By this time the sedative had started to work, and I was quite drowsy and not in much discomfort as the painkillers had also kicked in and were working on settling the cramping in my tummy. It was not very nice.

The lovely vet Emily also took my temperature and checked I was hydrated and not lacking in fluids. She gave The Blind Chick another little syringe of stuff to put over my tongue if the tummy ache persisted in four hours, but I didn't have to have another lot of medicine. That was good. So slowly but surely, I felt much better and my tummy ache was gone.

The lovely vet Emily thought I may have had sand colic, but The Blind Chick is very careful where she feeds me, normally on the grass and I am fed my hard feed in a big tub on the ground so I can't spill it on the ground and get dirt or sand in my tummy. But the vet still seems to think I could've had a dose of sand colic, being in a drought you pull everything up by the roots, so I probably had a tummy full of sand.

The vet suggested to The Blind Chick the next day to give me another dose of psyllium husks to help move any sand that may have been in my tummy. She added a little bit of molasses to sweeten it for me as I was not very keen on the stuff. But with the molasses it was yum. It smelt a little bit like liquorice, and I love liquorice. So, I ate it all up. We go through this process now every couple of months just to make sure there is not a build-up of sand in my tummy because it does make you very, very sick.

But two days later you wouldn't have even known I had a tummy ache. Everything was back to normal and I was back in work. But I know it gave the blind chickie babe a very big scare, and she is so very conscious of putting my feed on the grass so I don't get sand in my tummy and also feeding me in a rubber tub so that I can't spill my feed on the ground. It is so easy for a horse to get sand in their tummy and a dose of colic. If not caught early, colic can kill a horse and I think this was in her mind all the time. She did not want to lose me.

14.
Furry friends

Since I have moved to my new home, I've also made a couple of new friends. One of them is Matt and The Blind Chick's cat Thunder Paws. He is rather a cool dude, he is a very fluffy, light ginger, cream and white Persian type cat. He has lots and lots of fur and he has a little bit of an attitude as well. He sits on the veranda and watches The Blind Chick and I in the paddock and when we are out at the dressage arena, he is waiting under the pine trees observing what we are up to. He is a little bit like The Blind Chick's shadow, but he is very wary of her. Because she can't see him, she treads on him a lot. So outside he watches from a distance and not too keen to let The Blind Chick approach him, as he realises she can't see and she treads on him. Poor Thunder Paws. But he loves her dearly. At night he sleeps with The Blind Chick and Matt and has lots of cuddles. He's a bit of a cool dude as I said.

My other little mate is a Cavoodle. A Cavalier cross Miniature Poodle. Her name is Bonnie. She belongs to Matthew's mum and dad Lee and John and she is the love of their life. Bonnie is rather a pretty little thing. She likes coming down and helping herself to my manure in the paddock which doesn't mind me, but I don't think Lee and John like her eating and rolling in my manure. It makes her breath stink I would think.

I often see Matthew with Bonnie on the motorbike. Bonnie sitting in front of Matthew on the fuel tank with her ears flapping like Dumbo the elephant. She loves going on the motorbike with Matt and when he is out ploughing the paddocks, she is in the cab of the tractor sitting in the air conditioning with him. She is one very clever little puppy.

When Lee and John go on holidays, Bonnie is Matt's shadow. He calls her the French Kelpie because of her being a cavalier poodle cross. I don't know what Bonnie would do if she ever saw a sheep. I know she loves chasing the foxes and any little wallabies that come into the yard. She makes one hell of a noise.

Then there is Thunder Paws's partner in crime Sarge, the beautiful ginger cat who lives next door with Lee and John. Sarge is quite an independent character, quite a large ginger cat with an extremely long tail. He pokes around the garden looking for mice, stalks the odd pigeon but is never quick enough to catch one.

In winter you often catch the three fur babies, Thunder Paws, Sarge and Bonnie sitting on the veranda together enjoying the sunshine and each other's company. They often play tag in the garden, rumbling and rolling with each other. They are really very, very cute. They don't often venture into my yard; well Bonnie does, to pick up poo. But that's about it. Thunder Paw sits at the gate and waits for The Blind Chick when she feeds me. It's a pretty cool existence here. Nice animals and nice next-door neighbours Ben and Sophie.

I have noticed during the last few months when it has been so very hot, Thunder Paws has spent more time inside in the air conditioning. What a clever pussycat. But he also gets bites on his ears from the mosquitoes, so I tend to think The Blind Chick and Matt are keeping him inside, so he doesn't get bites all over him.

Thunder Paws and Sarge also keep a close eye on the tack shed for any little mice running around. Both of them are very good mousers, and Bonnie is pretty quick. Also, Bonnie has been known to take the mice off Sarge and eat them in front of him, what a meanie.

15.
Maintenance

Well one of the most important things is to get your saddle fitted every twelve months. In my case, The Blind Chick brought me a new saddle five months ago, a lovely Prestige dressage saddle. In the past five months, my shape has changed because of my training. I now have muscles where I didn't used to have muscles. Time to go and see Jason from Trail Race Saddlery, who is a professional saddle fitter and he will refit my saddle so it fits perfectly.

Well it has been a world wind trip down to Somersby where I had the honour of staying at the beautiful Alex Martin's property surrounded by beautiful foals. I wanted to pop one in the float and bring it home with me.

But the main reason for the trip wasn't for me to bring home a beautiful little foal. But to have my saddle re-fitted because I have changed shape again since Jason fitted my brand-new Prestige saddle six months ago. I have had a major, major transformation. More muscle. More beautiful top line.

So, we arrived at the lovely Alex's, and 15 minutes after we arrived the A-Team turned up from Trail Race Saddlery at Tuggerah. The A-Team being Steve and Jason Phillips who are master saddle fitters. So, I had them working on me and my saddle to get everything just right. Steve did a little bit of work on the saddle when they were there, then took the saddle home and did more work on it. The next morning, he brought the saddle back all ready to go. Time for The Blind Chick to take it home and see how it went.

The Blind Chick is very grateful for the time that Jason and Steve spent explaining to her what they were doing with refitting my saddle. They got her to feel where the contact was and wasn't and where the saddle needed more flocking. It was really wonderful, and she had a great understanding of how the changes would make such a difference to the saddle. It felt very nice on my back, and much more balanced after the boys had worked with it. So, it will be awesome to see how it goes when The Blind Chick rides in it.

Well it's nearly Thursday again, every six weeks Jeffrey a wonderful farrier comes out to put new shoes on me. It is imperative that I get shod every six weeks so my hooves don't get too long.

When Jeffrey first gets here, he has a bit of a chat with The Blind Chick about how I have been travelling. If I have been tripping or if I have had any health issues like abscesses or thrush in my hooves. Then he can work out a plan of attack if he needs to manage my hooves any differently.

Jeffrey generally takes all my shoes off first and then dresses them. Dressing means giving them a rasp and tidying them up. Sometimes he needs to take a little more hoof off, as my hooves grow quite well because I am on very nice pasture, good food and exceptional lucerne hay. As we all know, what we put in makes a very big difference to what our hooves do. If we want to make changes we need to feed the horse from inside. We can put oil on the hooves but this does not make a very big difference. It is what is put into our tummy that is converted to good healthy hooves.

While Jeffrey is tidying up my hooves, he has my new horse shoes in a very hot kiln heating them so he can make the shoes fit my whole hoof. It is really important that when you have a great Farrier like Jeffrey you ask lots of questions because he has all the answers and it is also very important not to make the hoof fit the shoe. The shoe has to be specially banged into shape to fit my particular hooves, as each hoof has its own individual shape and way that it grows.

The Blind Chick also feeds me a great product called Biotin, put out by our amazing sponsor Kelato. Biotin is really good for my hooves and helps them get stronger. It is also very good for your fingernails, so you can have Biotin to make your fingernails stronger.

Jeffrey takes a lot of time to make sure all my hooves are cut even and then he proceeds to shape the shoes to go on my hooves and I am then shod. Jeffrey shoes me with hot shoes, which is called hot shoeing. Some people prefer to have shoes not put on their horse hot, but I think it gives the shoe a good seat on my foot as it is slightly burnt into the hoof.

My hooves are generally quite nice and soft as my paddock is irrigated so my feet don't dry out too much which makes shoeing much easier. After I am shod, I am put in the paddock and I get the next day off. This is one of The Blind Chicks' things. She generally doesn't ride the day after I am shod. She lets me get used to my new shoes.

Next week I hear we have the Equine Dentist coming to do my teeth. This is a yearly event and the dentist generally comes and checks my teeth to make sure I don't have any sharp edges or any teeth that need to come out. Also, this helps with how the bit fits in my mouth. The Equine Dentist generally does what they call a bit seat and this makes the bit sit quite nicely in my mouth.

Just a little hint, you can generally tell if your horses teeth need doing if they are dropping quite a bit of feed out of their mouth when they are eating.

This process of having my teeth done generally takes about an hour to do. It doesn't hurt, but it's just a little uncomfortable. They put a gag in your mouth to hold your mouth open, and then they do some rasping to make sure you don't have any rough edges. My mouth feels much better after they have done my teeth, and I must say, I am able to chew a lot easier. So glad my teeth get done once a year.

But I did hear that The Blind Chick does not like the dentist very much and she gets my teeth done more often than she gets her own looked at. Need to do something about this I think.

It seems to be the month for maintenance February. I also have a visit from a local vet to give me my tetanus and strangles injection. As much as I must say needles aren't my favourite thing, I think getting a needle for tetanus is much better than getting tetanus itself. This injection is given each year with the strangles injection. Strangles is also a thing that I would not like to get, so the needle is a great preventative and seeing we do a bit of travelling to different showground stables, it will help with me not getting this horrible disease.

The other thing which is very, very big in my maintenance program is my Equissage Therapy. Every day before I get ridden I get this amazing machine put on my back like a saddle. It has lots of different settings for different massages. While I am having my massage with my back pad, The Blind Chick gives me a massage with the handheld device on my neck and my shoulders on both sides, up between my ears, around my poll, then moves to the back of my body and does the top of my back, my hamstrings and all of those big muscles. This is such a relaxing thing to have done before I get ridden. They say the massage is equivalent to a twenty-minute warmup. This is much more pleasant than a twenty-minute warmup. I can tell you after the Equissage Therapy I don't feel like going and working. I feel so relaxed and wonderful. Wouldn't mind nodding off to sleep.

After my Equissage is taken off I am given a lovely brush and settled and taken out to the dressage arena. In fact, I take The Blind Chick out to the dressage arena. She mounts and we do a twenty-minute walk warmup with lots of flexing and suppling. Because the Equissage machine does such a great job relaxing me, all of my muscles are soft and supple to start with, which is great.

Then there are a couple of other things that happen later in the year, which is because I get quite a hairy coat. The Blind Chick organises for somebody to come and clip me and make me look all shiny and shorthaired again. Sometimes she has a bit of a go, but there is generally a fairly big mess to clean up, because she misses a bit. But it makes the job quicker for the friend that comes and clips me for her, and I must say I look terribly sexy after I have been clipped. Before I have been clipped I look a little bit like a woolly mammoth.

The other thing The Blind Chick is really passionate about, is having my paddocks quite clear of weeds. After rain the Cat Head and the Khaki Weed get a bit out of control. So, she generally gets her husband Matt to spray the paddocks out and we rest the paddock for 10 days before I can go back in. There is also a couple of weeds we should be looking out for after we have had some rain, there is a plant called Pig Weed which is quite deadly to horses if consumed over a long period of time, also Marshmallow Weed is not so good for us. Deadly Nightshade speaks for itself I think, and then there's the Heliotrope Family, not good.

So, it pays to be quite vigilant about what is growing in our paddocks. A little hard for The Blind Chick to do this, but she has lots of great mates that let her know when the weeds are coming away and also Matt is really on the ball with the weed spraying system.

Another thing, and in some people's cases they don't see it as a biggie, but I love clean drinking water. So, The Blind Chick washes my water trough out at least once a week, and with these horrible dust storms we have been getting, it is so appreciated. The water gets very dirty and yucky very quickly.

One of the other things that The Blind Chick has high on her "must get done" list is the arena being groomed. But her wonderful husband does that for her with the tractor. She has to pull the arena down, and then he grooms the arena. Afterwards, Matthew will help The Blind Chick put the arena up. When Matthew helps it takes twenty minutes. When The Blind Chick does it by herself it takes two hours. So, she really appreciates the help putting the arena back up.

Oh, here's the other thing, The Blind Chick is a bit passionate about is the gear being cleaned. Generally, in summer I have a clean rug each day as she hates me being uncomfortable or in a dirty rug. In winter I get a week out of a rug because I have another rug on top to protect me from the wind and rain. But having clean gear on me is really important as it also stops rubs and itches.

She also washes my saddle cloth and girth every couple of days, and I must say I do appreciate this. There is nothing more horrible than a crusty old saddle cloth being put on with a crusty old girth. It feels horrible! So, when I have clean gear put on me I am definitely happier.

I must say in some ways The Blind Chick must sound a bit pedantic, but it is all for my comfort. She is also very diligent about my bridle being soft and oiled and the bit being cleaned each day after it has been in my mouth. She also maintains her saddle beautifully by oiling it at least a couple of times a week. Keeping it nice and clean. This is no mean feat seeing we have had so much dust and horrible weather.

The Blind Chick and I are pretty lucky to have some great sponsors that keep me looking and feeling wonderful. At my new home in Dubbo, it is very hot. We had three and a bit weeks over forty degrees. This was really, really hard on my body, but I was able to cope so well because of all the supplements that The Blind Chick gives me.

Well starting with one of the main things, The Blind Chick uses a wonderful electrolyte which I think is ideal in this extreme heat. She uses the amazing electrolyte replacer KelatoLYTE which helps me keep very hydrated, and also keeps me drinking.

The other thing which I think is paramount is my gut health.

Without a good gut, well nothing goes right! So, The Blind Chick has been using the amazing GastroAID supplement with me since she bought me. This makes me feel so healthy, and on top of the world all the time.

In fact, not meaning to brag … but if you have a look at the pictures, I do look like a little bit of a fine specimen. Even if I do say so myself.

One of the other things which I also put in the top three supplements is my hoof care supplement. Without feet you have no horse. The Blind Chick has been using Kelato BiotinMAX Concentrate. It is a must. My hooves are healthy and this is also a reflection of my gut health. It's all a little bit of a vicious circle. We need to look after the whole body and be quite holistic about our approach.

The other thing The Blind Chick cares a lot about is my joints. From the moment she bought me, she's been using the wonderful Kelato NutriFLEX. It is paramount with a horse my size that you look after the joints. Especially considering my workload. Working at Medium, Advanced level dressage. It's just so important to have great health in my joints.

Now for my favourite type of maintenance, this looks after my mind and my body and it is an amazing treatment given by a wonderful friend Tanya Hind. I have my Craniosacral Therapy every two weeks which is just divine.

My wonderful therapist Tanya is here and the blind chickie is filling her in about our time away and what new training techniques she has just learned whilst away. I am very patient as you are all aware, but this morning is about me and my time with Tanya. So, I just poked my nose in and gave her some nudges to let her know that I am here and ready to start.

I know you are all wondering what this Craniosacral Therapy does for me, so I will try to explain how it feels and what it does to my body. To start with Tanya puts her gentle hands on my back to assess the Craniosacral rhythm in my body. This is the rhythm made by the fluid that runs from my brain to the tip of my tail and back. It is through this that Tanya can feel which parts of my body have blockages that cause me to become stiff, sore and sometimes quite unbalanced.

I really feel for other horses that do not have my lovely Tanya to release these blockages because when these are left, things just become worse. Us equines just shift the pain around from limb to limb until we cannot do so anymore.

The other thing that I love about this lady is that she listens to what I am telling her. She has this intuitive way of understanding everything that I am saying. She has even had a vision of one of my accidents. This really blows the mind of the blind chickie. But not me. I know what she is capable of and I trust her all the way.

Today I have led Tanya to my left shoulder even though I know she can feel that I have a slight blockage in my withers. She puts her hands just next to my scapular and connects to the tissues around and underneath my scapular. I can feel her connect in with my energy and then the tingling begins. For a first timer this would be a weird feeling. But I know that is the sign of my tissues releasing and relaxing under her hands, so I stand still until finally the muscle and fascia around my scapular release. It is at this point that I start to lick and chew as things let go. My body also shifts, and as it does

I have to move with it as things become relaxed and move back into their natural alignment.

Today I was able to relax even further than I have before. It is something that you would all enjoy. Tanya takes you to a place of peace and tranquillity. As I allow the tingling to run throughout my body, Tanya's hands are still on my scapular. I have to stretch my back legs, my back, my neck and shoulder. Without even thinking my body has just done a full-on cat stretch, yawned and then let out the biggest breath from my nostrils. WOW! I just love that feeling when things drop back into place.

Now you are reading this thinking that this all just happens. But let me assure you some fascia muscle or nerves that have been traumatised and that I have in turn switched off from my brain to be able to keep functioning through without the pain, are very difficult to release. I have to move about quite a bit to get through this intense vibration and sometimes shooting pain in my body. It is just lucky Tanya can also feel my pain and keeps her hands with me, even when I am shaking my head up and down vigorously to release the tension. Tanya is such a patient human and comforts me all the way through with soft encouraging verbal cues. Without her I would not be able to release the tensions in my body, I know that for a fact.

I can feel the tingling again over the top of my scapular which is the blood flowing back into the muscle in a bigger volume than has been getting to it for some time. I can hear Tanya telling the blind chickie that she can feel the tissue becoming plump under her hands. As this is continuing to happen I am stretching my hind leg as well. So much of my body is closely connected to the other by the fascia, a thin web like layers of tissue that covers the muscles and cartridge of the whole body. By releasing one area of my body the fascia ensures it then releases another, as the fascia is the connection between them all.

So, my left shoulder is now free and I can feel the tissue gliding back and forth even though I am not actually moving my leg. Tanya has also felt this and I am now guiding her to the right shoulder and much the same as the other, it took some time to release. But, I got through it with the help of my trusty therapist. Now I have been waiting for an opportunity for Tanya to be able to work on my C6, C7 and T1 vertebrae, and now is the time. Tanya is following my lead again and directing the energy that I need to release these. Oh, this feels soooo good! I am just sinking into that tranquil place again whilst she does her magic. It is a very difficult joint to get to as it is right in the middle of my scapular bones deep in my chest so I am helping her out as best I can and allowing the energy to flow down and around my sternum area.

Tanya has also directed the energy flow to the cartilage that runs along the bottom of my rib cage and back up into my sternum on each side. This is important to keep nice and free so that I can move freely through my gaits and turns. I am just so relaxed at the present. I don't really want to leave this state. I am licking and chewing again and the tension has gone from the bottom of my neck and shoulder area. All of this work has made me itchy. It's time for me to have a scratch before I continue with the session.

Ok, now my nuchal ligament is quite tight. This is the very strong ligament along the top of my neck that assists me with my self-carriage among other things. I was feeling a bit of tightness. Tanya has put her hands in just the right place to get the cerebrospinal fluid pumping again.

Now she tells me we have the hard part. Tanya tries to place her hands on my ears to target the nerves just at the base of my ears that connect to other parts of my body and my brain. I can feel her hands coming toward my ears and I know that she isn't going to hurt me, but I just cannot bear the direct contact. So, I put my head up as high as I can. At eighteen hands high, she cannot reach my ears, so just as her hands make contact they slide off. She tries again and I do the same. Tanya does not get angry, she just lets me know it will be ok. She is usually right about these things, so I let her make contact just for a moment. The sparks that I feel are a bit overwhelming, so I put my head up again. Eventually I can hang in there long enough for my number 2,6,7 and 8 nerves to be released. This was not easy for me at all, but I did it. Tanya was so happy with me. As you can imagine with the nerves connecting to other regions of my body I did a lot of stretching, chewing and yawning as these released themselves. The relief that I felt was astronomical. My body just melted.

My head stall had come loose during the session and fell off at this point. But I am not going anywhere. Just a little more please Tanya! To finish off the session I stood right where I was in the yard as Tanya checked my craniosacral rhythm to make sure all was back in balance. Then she disengaged from my energy field ever so gently as if she was never there.

I feel so refreshed after my treatment. I think the therapy loosens everything up and gets everything back in equilibrium. My favourite time of the month is when Tanya visits. Also, after the treatment, The Blind Chick gives me the day off. When I come back into work, I get an easy day. The Blind Chick focuses on getting my body to feel its way and does lots of stretches and lots of suppling exercises. This is greatly appreciated. Especially now with our new way of training with José. This is just awesome.

16.
My blind chick

One of The Blind Chicks' good mates Bob Cooper wrote this about her and I thought it was worth sharing before I begin.

She lives in constant shadows, the darkness of the night,
But strength is her companion in the ever-fading light,
Sue may be blind to others, she is not blind to me,
For I have found her secret, that my friend Sue can see.
Though eyesight may elude her, I have known it from the start,
She doesn't need the eyesight, for Sue sees with her heart.
Her sense of hearing, smell and touch, are sharpened by her plight,
Her kind deeds and compassion, have kept her from the night.
And no complaints are offered, affliction is her shield,
A knight in shining armour, upon life's battle field.
We lose our way, we rarely hear the song bird in the tree,
And often we blunder through life with things we will not see.
Her great love for her animals, her courage through each trial,
Her great determination, still leaves me with a smile,
I know that others call her blind, it matters not to me,
For I have found her secret, that my friend Sue can see.
For Sue my hero.
—Coop 2013 RIP

Well I thought it fair to give you a little bit of a background on my blind chick. She is also writing a book. But her book will come out after mine. Her story and her journey are definitely worth a mention.

She was born on a lovely property in Mudgee called "Kaludabah." The property was 21,000 acres, and I tend to think when I listen to her telling stories she spent most of her time roaming the hills on her beautiful horse and only coming home of an evening for dinner. Just loved being by herself and with her ponies.

Really, to be very truthful I don't think very much has changed. She is still the kid at heart. She loves bareback rides. Loves just sitting in the paddock with me and having a chat, going for walks. I think she misses the fact that she can't just take me out for a ride in the paddock by herself. But we spend pretty amazing quality time together in that dressage arena, and also riding bareback, which she gets a real kick out of.

The Blind Chick has had a lot of horses that have taken her many places and achieved many, many goals. She had a lovely stallion called Yarrahappini Hectic which she won Highpoints Horse of Australia at Chinchilla in the early 90s. What an accomplishment when you can't see, and the trust she must have had with her beautiful stallion Hecco. She talks of him fondly and often.

She has tried her hand at most things. She loved show jumping as a kid. Apparently, she never opened gates. Just went over the rail between the ramp and the gate, keeping in mind generally this was done bareback. She loved going around her cross-country course on her beautiful mare Silver which was her father's station horse, bareback, no bridle, no saddle round the cross-country course. Just total trust in her horse, and this hasn't left her. This yearning for the trust, to stay a kid and to keep that love of a horse just like a kid. It's fun. It makes her smile.

Little did The Blind Chick know that her bond with her beautiful horses would qualify her to represent Australia at no less than two Paralympic Games, Atlanta in 1996 and the Sydney 2000 Paralympic Games. She also represented Australia at the World Equestrian Games in 1999 where she won the Bronze Medal, and was ranked Fourth in the World.

The most amazing thing about these three international competitions is that the horses were drawn out of a hat, and the competitors got to ride the horses just three days before the competition, for only 45 minutes before they represented their country. This is pretty amazing when you think how special the bond is between a horse and rider. When you are blind or you have any disability that bond and that knowledge is imperative. I know The Blind Chick thinks it is rather wonderful these days that the Para-equestrians are allowed to use their own horses and things are much more on an even playing field now.

One of the other things The Blind Chick has had is six Guide Dogs over 38 years. She received her first Guide Dog in 1984, and her last Guide Dog Amani retired in 2019. She no longer has a guide dog. These amazing animals have given her the most awesome independence and she has travelled the world with them. All of these things will be explored more in depth in her book I am sure.

I am just going over a few highlights, things that I can remember off the top of my head. The other thing I know The Blind Chick was very proud about, was being an Australia Day Ambassador for 21 years. Each year going to a different town, or up to 5 towns in one day, speaking about her journey, what she has accomplished, how proud she is of being an Australian citizen and what a lucky country we live in. We are truly blessed.

She was also appointed to the board of the Sydney Paralympics by the honourable Michael Knight after the Atlanta Paralympics. This was an amazing experience for a country kid, and I'm sure as you know The Blind Chick is pretty shy, but she settled in to being a part of the board of the Sydney Paralympics really well. She loved her time there. Met so many amazing people.

While we're on the subject of the Paralympic Games, I think her highlight with the Paralympic Games, apart from the fact that she was representing her country, Australia, she met some of the most amazing beautiful people. Other Paralympians who had the most amazing stories, and had also been on an awesome journey. They used to sit of an evening outside the living quarters and listen to stories, The Blind Chick and her then guide dog Eccles loved these evenings.

Another one of the things The Blind Chick has excelled at, has been doing long distance rides. There have been ten of these long-distance rides which have always been over many hundreds of kilometres. Sometimes thousands of kilometres.

Doing these rides with her has always been her trusty little Australian stock horse mare Mudgee, apart from her last one. Mudgee passed away at the ripe old age of 35. But while Mudgee was alive she did nine of the long-distance rides with The Blind Chick and the rest of her team. She generally had six other horses on the rides, generally Australian Stockhorses, and had an amazing team of supporters. She is always supported by one sighted guide, a support vehicle and truck drivers. It was quite a feat to organise and coordinate all of these events.

The Blind Chick's dad did all the rides with her, except for her last ride. He passed away in 2010. He was her hero. I often hear her tell her friends about how he never said no, he always supported her, and it was never an excuse not to have a go because you are blind. I tend to think she was very blessed to have had such a wonderful father.

Her dad's Lions Club also had a lot to do with the long-distance rides, as the Mudgee Lions Club was the charity that coordinated the events in the towns they travelled through. They also dispersed the money to the charity that The Blind Chick was riding for.

To give you an idea of some of the rides, and just what they achieved; Canberra to the Gold Coast in 1988, 2400 kilometres, 56 days in the saddle and raising $77,000 for Riding For The Disabled Mudgee. This is one of the ten rides. I know another ride that she is very proud of which was a ride from Melbourne to Sydney for the Sydney Paralympic games. That ride raised $1.1 million and was 1200 kilometres. What an amazing achievement. She has helped and made a difference to so many peoples' lives. If I had a hat, I would take my hat off to The Blind Chick.

Her last long-distance ride was to raise money for the Oncology Unit in her home town Dubbo at the Dubbo Base Hospital. This ride was very different, as in she didn't use her usual Australian Stockhorses. She used all Australian Thoroughbreds off the track. Quite a few of her friends, Jana, Joe and Jenelle took horses to train for the ride. The Blind Chick had two beautiful Godolphin horses to train, their names were Vasco, a lovely bay gelding, and the beautiful Spilsbury, a beautiful black gelding.

The Blind Chick would get friends to come out and ride with her and do miles around Matthews paddocks to get the miles up on the horses, and the other girls did the same. Got the horses fit for the long-distance ride. It was only a short-ride, 700 kilometres and they raised just under $80,000. What a team effort for the Oncology Unit at Dubbo Base Hospital.

The other thing The Blind Chick has done is trained up quite a few horses through dressage. There has been a natural progression into the dressage arena. Being totally blind, it keeps her safe and we know where she is.

Can't say the same for The Blind Chick, because she generally never knows where she is. But with the backing of her beautiful horses they look after her and guide her around the dressage arena and allow her to do beautiful dressage tests. This is also accomplished by the generosity of her wonderful friends who are her living markers. They stand at the letter and call the letters. She relies on her hearing in the dressage arena, not sight.

She has trained quite a few of these horses up to Grand Prix level. But she had never had the opportunity to ride at that level. Enter an amazing gentleman into her life called Terry Snow and his wonderful family. They sponsored The Blind Chick for four years with that other horse she had, Desiderata, and she got to do a dressage display at Grand Prix level at Dressage by The Sea at Willinga Park. It was such a highlight and would never ever have been accomplished if it wasn't for the amazing generosity and support of the Snow family and her awesome team of living markers and friends.

Then bring on the next chapter of her life which is me, the amazing Johno. The Blind Chick and I are having such a spectacular journey learning so much. The trust that we have together is building every day.

17.
José Mendez, Classical Dressage

Well I should've picked up there was something happening on Sunday. The Blind Chick was buzzing around like a little bee and I must say I did notice the float parked up near the tack shed. I was also brought up and given a bath and a bit of a trim. This definitely sparked my curiosity. There was definitely something about to happen.

Early the next morning, the blind chickie babe toddled on down to feed me at six in the morning! She generally feeds me at seven. This I thought was also a bit peculiar. But I went with the flow, had my breakfast and a biscuit of hay. Then, The Blind Chick came down and put floating boots on me, gave me a brush and put a light rug on me for travelling. So, it looks like today we were off on a road trip.

Karen arrived at around eight, and came down and got me out of the paddock. She led me up to the tack shed. A little bit of fly spray was put on me to keep the bugs away while we were travelling and I was on the float in no time at all. The float was closed up with the back barn-doors left open for airflow and all the windows opened to keep me cool. While we were travelling I had no idea where we were going. I thought no one has told me. No one has confided in me, or asked me if I even wanted to go on a road trip.

We travel for about four hours and then there was a break. The girls filled the Ranger up with fuel and got some lunch. I must say, I was a little impatient and started pawing in the float, so The Blind Chick came and ate her lunch with me to keep me pacified. God love me. I am a little bit precious. Well I know The Blind Chick loves me, in any case.

With lunch being over, we were off again. Another hour and a half down the road we quietly pulled up a country driveway and I had a quick peak out the window. All good, there are other horses here. I was unloaded and Karen led me to a paddock and gave me a biscuit of hay so I could have a relax for a while and have a drink after my long trip.

I noticed Karen and The Blind Chick talking to two people who ended up being very good friends of The Blind Chicks from years ago. It was the amazing master of classical dressage José Mendez and his beautiful wife Faye. They stood and talked for ages. Then The Blind Chick and Karen head off to Marulan to find their accommodation. They were staying at a lovely cottage in Marulan called Marulan Stays. The girls were staying in a fully self-contained and very comfortable little apartment. They said it smelt like it had just been all done up. Very comfortable indeed. So, the girls were settled, and so was I.

By the time The Blind Chick retuned, I had eaten all my hay and had a lovely big drink, plus met my next-door neighbours. A couple of very beautiful horses I must say. Karen came and got me out of my paddock while The Blind Chick got my work boots and brushes out to give me a brush. I was led up to the float and work boots put on but, no saddle, no bridle. What's going on here? We then walked over to the indoor arena where we were met again by José.

The girls had a good chat to José about what had been happening with my training, and then José took my halter off and put something on called a lunging cavesson. He also held a very long thin cane. I wondered what that was for.

He started working me on the long side of the dressage arena. Just walking and halting, walking and halting. Working on my response and getting my attention. Then he would stop and touch me under the belly very gently but persistently until my head dropped. And geewhiz, guess what, it was very relaxing this putting your head down and a big deep breath out felt great. This exercise was done quite a few times.

José then did some other exercises with me. Getting me to respond when he tapped my leg to lift my legs up. Working possibly more on my hind legs than on my front. I of course obliged. Karen had done some of these exercises earlier, so I was familiar with what José was wanting me to do. Then we started moving forward a little bit, doing half steps keeping, the rhythm and regularity.

This was just a lovely experience. No tension, no fuss. Just total relaxation all the time. When I did something really, really good I was given a treat by José and lots of praise and pats. Talk about knowing a way to a guy's heart. This José fella really knew what he was doing.

All the time these exercises were happening José was explaining to The Blind Chick what he was doing with me, why he was doing it, and the response he was expecting. She was totally in her element. I was responding, doing these quite difficult movements, and José hadn't had me in hand for more than twenty minutes. It was wonderful.

Well after my workout I was given a bit of a bath and a brush and popped in the paddock. Given my hard feed and a biscuit of hay and lots of cuddles, and of course my favourite carrots. The girls said their goodbyes to José and Faye and went back into town to have dinner and a quiet night.

The next morning the wonderful Faye brought me my breakfast and fed all the other horses. I had settled in really well. All my breakfast was gone when The Blind Chick and Karen turned up to come and get me for another lesson. Wow, what's today going to bring. It was so exciting. Yesterday The Blind Chick was so elated with what I had achieved with José. Bring on this lesson.

Okay everything happened the same as yesterday. My boots were put on, I was given a brush, feet cleaned out. But my saddle was put on this time. Okay, The Blind Chick must be going to ride today. Cool! But again, no bridle. I was walked over to the indoor arena where José was waiting for us. He took my halter off and then went and got the lunging cavesson and put it on me. We went in and did more exercises in hand. It was really cool. I remembered everything José taught me from the day before, so it was really, really easy.

We did lots of relaxation. I got lots of treats and José introduced a couple of other exercises which were the start of the passage movement. This was very cool and the lovely thing about it is the fact that The Blind Chick could pick up the fact that I had more elevation and suspension when I went past her. José did these exercises near The Blind Chick so she could hear what I was doing, also with José explaining. This made a big difference for her.

Then after my work in hand the bridle was put on and The Blind Chick got on. We walked around for a while. The Blind Chick got the feel of the arena and then José started his lesson. It was different than other lessons we had done. José works his circles on the clock face so this helped The Blind Chick with her orientation and knowing where she was. We were doing lateral work, shoulder in, half pass, pirouette. There it was. Really quite amazing. It took a little while for the penny to drop for her. But when it did, oh my god! You should have heard how ecstatic she was. Plus, being able to know where she was with the counting was just so cool.

We worked on our transitions, the positioning on the circle and keeping the circle. Again, lots of rewards and praise from The Blind Chick. We started with shoulder-in during the walk and using the positions on the clock to get the right angle. It totally rocked. Then we did some travers, and again using the numbers on the clock for The Blind Chick to know where she was in her movement. This was working a treat.

Also, all the time José was letting The Blind Chick know when she was going past the letters. He was calling out H when she rode past H. When she rode past S, he called out S. This gave her an awesome idea of where she was in the arena. He also helped her with counting the strides to go around the corner. Counting her strides is invaluable. She used to do it with her other horse, but my stride is much different than his. So, it takes a lot of work and a lot of concentration. But it was awesome

José said in time he will have The Blind Chick and I riding in the arena without him calling out the letters, as she will be counting in her head and know where she is. I think The Blind Chick is a little sceptical. But I put my money on José.

When the lesson was finished I was given lots of hugs and some treats. Then I was led over to the wash bay, given a good wash and a clean rug. Then I got to munch on a biscuit of hay back in my paddock for a relaxing afternoon.

That afternoon the girls came back and fed me and then headed back to Marulan to get dinner ready. José and Faye were coming for dinner. I have to tell you, The Blind Chick and Karen were very excited. They both had so many questions they wanted to ask José. This was a life changing experience in how to train with kindness and empathy and patience. If you happen to know The Blind Chick, patience isn't one of her big things. So, this is a biggie for her. So cool and working a treat.

Well, so I hear they had a wonderful night and both The Blind Chick and Karen learnt so much just listening to José's stories and talking with Faye. It was a wonderful night. The next day Faye brings me breakfast, feeding all of the other horses at the same time. I was wondering what time The Blind Chick and Karen were going to get here and what the day held in store for us.

The girls arrived and started cleaning up the float and hooking it onto the car so I thought we must be going home. I was really looking forward to my lesson today. Then another lovely lady called Lynn arrived. José did some work in hand with her beautiful horse and then Lyn had a lesson.

Wow, thank heavens we didn't leave this morning early. I was so relieved when Karen came and got me and took me over to the float and The Blind Chick put my work boots on, cleaned out my hooves and gave me a brush. We are having a lesson. Yes, this is too cool. Again, no bridle. Woohoo! I am going to be doing some more in hand work with the wonderful José. Let's see what magic we can get today.

Well the three of us walk over to the indoor arena and we were met by the wonderful José, who again took my halter off left me standing walked away did heaps of other things while I stood patiently in the arena. No halter or bridle. Oh boy! Oh boy! I'm a good lad. Then he got the lunging cavesson and put it on me. We were off doing some in hand work again.

Firstly, working on my straightness and my halts, making sure I halted square not leaving my hind leg behind me as I normally do. This was done with kindness and lots of praise and rewards. Then we did a little bit of Piaffe. While José, Faye, The Blind Chick and I were working down one end of the arena, Karen was in the arena listening and watching José, so she could learn what to do when we get home.

I hear in the background The Blind Chick saying, "Faye are you there? Could you please tell me what's happening?" Faye sat with The Blind Chick and explained to her what I was doing. I was doing some pretty handy piaffe apparently. Well, I tend to think The Blind Chick was just so excited. Then José did some piaffe down closer to The Blind Chick and she could hear my footsteps. The rhythm. The regularity. The softness. The kindness. My heavens, three days and look at I am doing. What a trainer.

Not an ounce of tension anywhere. We go around the arena another couple of times and then we go into the trot. José taps the front of my legs and I start lifting my legs higher as we shoot past The Blind Chick. I thought she was gonna burst her bubble. She was so, so very excited! I was doing the starts of a very, very nice passage. Beautiful rhythm. Beautiful regularity. Beautiful suspension. What more could a girl want? It felt so cool. José brought me back to a walk, then a halt. Lots of praise and a treat.

I tend to think The Blind Chick would've been happy to go home on that note. It was magic. All of these beautiful high-level movements accomplished in three days. Okay they are not established. But they are coming along beautifully. I am enjoying the journey. No pressure, no tension, no stress. I so want to please José and The Blind Chick.

The day before The Blind Chick asked José whether he would like to have a ride on me. He said he would love it, and it would be an honour to ride me. So next thing José is getting on my back.

Wow! What a kind, understanding, passionate rider. José did everything with kindness, working on the rhythm and regularity. The transitions, just all the simple things that make a great dressage horse. José dismounted and said I was rather wonderful. I think The Blind Chick knows that. But it was really cool coming from José, who is a master.

Then, The Blind Chick gets on. She had been thinking of all of the wonderful things José had taught us the day before. It came easier for her today, and heaven help us. We had a couple of other people there watching, but that didn't seem to worry The Blind Chick. She just got on with business. It was so cool. The shoulder-in came easier, the travers was easier, the canter transitions were so soft and uphill. It was an absolute ripper of a lesson.

All the time José letting The Blind Chick know where she was in the arena. Where the corners were. It must've been exhausting for him. It's not like giving a sighted person a lesson, where they can see the letters, corners and where they are in the arena. He did a magic job and we didn't run into anything.

I tend to think the whole time throughout the lesson, the smile did not move off The Blind Chick's face. You could hear in her voice the elation, the enjoyment, and how much easier it was on day three. It was such a cool lesson.

Well after the lesson everybody said how wonderful I was, and that I was so easy to teach. I try very hard to please The Blind Chick and José. It's amazing what happens with kindness, love and of course the odd treat. I must say, that is a bit of a game changer. I love my treats.

After the lesson my gear was taken off, I was given a bath, a light rug put on for travelling and I was put back in the paddock so I could have a drink and a relax little before we hit the road to drive back to Dubbo. The Blind Chick and Karen went and said their goodbyes to José and Faye. They came and got me out of my paddock, Karen put me on the float The Blind Chick shut the back bar. The barn doors are left open for airflow and we are off, on the road back to Dubbo.

I think I slept most of the way home. But I have to tell you, watching the girls in the front of the car, they did not stop talking and laughing all the way home. Talking about the lesson. Talking about what they had learnt from the amazing José. Talking about our next trip down for more lessons. Must say, I can't wait. I know the girls are very excited to get back down for more lessons. Classical dressage, bring it on!

18.
Thank you Facebook friends

I think it would be very remiss of me if I didn't mention our Facebook friends for lots of reasons. The fact that you have always taken time to respond to my posts, you have always helped build up The Blind Chick when she is feeling down, or when she's feeling a little bit down, lacking confidence or anxious.

It is amazing what a kind word, or the fact that someone can say "I'm going through the same thing" or "we believe in you" makes an amazing difference. Sometimes, as you could imagine, it is pretty difficult when you are totally blind getting to know a new horse, riding by yourself in an arena, not knowing where you are, and sometimes I am sure the confidence thing gives her a little bit of a rattle and can cause some anxiety. You have all helped The Blind Chick to get over that, and also some very special people who she has met through Facebook have really helped back her up. The podcast by the wonderful Jane Pike and her "itty-bitty shitty committee" about how we can sometimes let our minds feed us rubbish. Thank you, Jane for giving The Blind Chick the skills, just by listening to a podcast, to get rid of the "itty-bitty shitty committee" who are trying to undermine her in her head. It was so cool.

The Blind Chick's beautiful friend Cathy Price from Wales, who she rings and talks to on the phone. Cathy is always sending her beautiful love and me too of course. She so believes in us. It is wonderful.

Then, there are just all of the other beautiful people who just bother to be kind. Who enjoy following our journey. Who give us feedback. Who make us feel wonderful. We so appreciate you all. I am so grateful for all your help with the writing of my book. I tend to think I would have never been able to decide on a title for the book without my Facebook friends.

So, from the bottom of my heart, thank you all beautiful Facebook friends that follow Johno and The Blind Chick. Thank you for your love and support. Thank you for believing in us. I tend to think I would have not written my book if it wasn't for you. I am sure The Blind Chick would not be writing her book, if it wasn't for you as well. You have given us both the confidence and encouragement to share our journey. Thank you from the bottom of both our hearts.

So, in true Johno fashion;

Loads of love and hugs,

Johno and the Blind Chick

19.
A great opportunity

Well things apparently at the moment are going a little haywire in the human world. There is a virus out there called the coronavirus. It has the ability to make the elderly and very young very sick. So, at the moment the country is in a little bit of a dilemma and not sure where to go or what to do.

There have been some lockdowns with travel. But I think this is just the beginning. We were planning on being down at José Mendez for training this week, but because of the coronavirus we decided not to do this trip. To make sure that we did not bring any virus back with us or be seen to be doing the wrong thing. It is important to be responsible.

So, we have decided to be responsible at home. It is a wonderful opportunity for The Blind Chick to consolidate and work on her relationship with me. It must be so difficult forming a relationship with a new horse. New stride, new personality, the whole bit. It must be just quite daunting. I know that The Blind Chick still struggles some days with the "itty-bitty shitty committee", the voice inside her head trying to undermine her and making her feel anxious. So, this time for us to be in semi lockdown is a wonderful opportunity for us to work hard on our relationship and moving forward.

I know there was another thing The Blind Chick would have liked to have achieved with me this year. That is going out and competing. But she has been very wise and considerate about us building a solid relationship and her knowing me 100%.

But this hasn't stopped the questions; "when are you going out with Johno?" "What are you doing with Johno?" "When are you going to be taking Johno to a competition?" "Are you going to Dressage By The Sea?" It all would've been lovely to have done all of the above but, The Blind Chick is not ready to go out and compete yet.

We need to consolidate our relationship, and The Blind Chick must be much more comfortable and confident when doing movements. If there is the slightest bang or I lose my attention for a milli second and she feels tension she just freezes. This makes me think; "oh, my heavens what's wrong? I need to be scared now!" So, it is a little bit counter intuitive. With one getting a fright and then one feeding off the other.

So, it is important to work on The Blind Chick's confidence before we go out. We also have our dressage arena marker announcers to do work with. This is going to be a very big project over the next few weeks. We need to consolidate and get that working really well. Whether we take that out to compete will be another thing. With the living markers The Blind Chick uses, it is much quieter than with the dressage arena marker announcer. But we shall continue to practice and work out which is the best way to go.

The Blind Chick's goal is to go out later this year. Possibly the local dressage club's event. We are so lucky to have the Orana Equestrian Club run events year-round. She is thinking of the event over the

October long weekend. But if we don't achieve this goal, it doesn't matter. We are building on our relationship every day and our movements are getting better. Really all that matters is that The Blind Chick is happy and loving what she does.

So, here's to that wonderful opportunity we have. To consolidate, to build on, to improve on, all aspects of our relationship. Hopefully, by the end of the year we will be in the dressage arena competing.

I really hope you have enjoyed reading about our journey so far. In April 2020, The Blind Chick and I have spent one whole year together. It has been the most amazing year of my life. I have learnt about life with a blind chick. I have learnt to love and respect and please somebody. It is the most important thing to me to make The Blind Chick happy. I know she is working on everything she can do to keep our training kind and ask not tell and fun which is the main thing because I know she does this dressage stuff and rides me because she loves doing it. For no other reason.

Keep an eye out in April 2020 for our two-year anniversary book!

So please give us feedback on the book. Please let us know if there's anything we have missed out that you would like to know in our next book.

Happy riding everybody!

Loads of love and hugs,

Johno and the Blind Chick

The story continues in

JOHNO
and the Blind Chick

Part 2

Coming 2021

Follow Johno on Facebook for updates.
www.facebook.com/JohnoAndTheBlindChick/

Acknowledgements

Without a doubt, the most massive acknowledgement of appreciation goes to The Blind Chick's husband Matthew, for having a vision and believing in me.

The amazing Yana Poppy, for encouraging me to tell this story and keep sharing the journey.

The amazing and awesome Emily Blackburne for having the imagination and the patience for deciphering the gobbledygook whenever I sent new chapters to her.

My wonderful brains trust, The Blind Chick's mother-in-law Lee Manny, for being part of Matthew buying me and also for her guidance with the book and being the first person (apart from Emily) to read my book.

To these two amazing ladies I am indebted for putting the book together and helping it make sense. Totally, ever so grateful.

To our more than amazing friends on Facebook. Your support, your encouragement, your belief in *Johno and The Blind Chick* has been amazing and so much appreciated. You have guided, you have suggested and you have been a major part of this journey. Thank you from the bottom of my heart.

Also, a massive thank you to Belinda Crawford who saved us. I was struggling. I had no idea where to turn or what to do and this amazing lady has taken the book the rest of the way by doing the front cover, typesetting and getting it to the publishers. Thank you lovely lady. You truly rock and you saved my hide.

A special thank you to The Blind Chick's niece Sarah for her artistic talent and moral support.

To our beautiful and talented photographer Prue Crichton, thank you so much for your beautiful photos and for allowing us to use them in my book. You're so gratefully appreciated.

To our wonderful friend Lyndal Oatley, triple Olympian, advocate against bullying and all-round beautiful lady, thank you for endorsing my book. I am honoured, privileged and grateful for your beautiful words and honesty. Thank you from the bottom of my heart.

To our wonderful readers, hope you enjoy our journey. Be kind!

Loads of love and hugs,

Johno.

Sue-Ellen Lovett is a motivational speaker, two-time Paralympian and Grand Prix-level dressage rider. She's also blind, but she hasn't let that slow her down.

Born with a degenerative eye disease that left her legally blind from birth and without sight for the last decade, Sue-Ellen has a slew of awards, and has competed against able-bodied riders at the highest level of international competition. In 1996, Sue-Ellen competed in the Atlanta Paralympic Games, following it up by competing in the Sydney Paralympic Games four years later, and a four-year stint on the Sydney Paralympic Board of Directors.

In between Atlanta and Sydney Paralympic Games, she represented Australia at the World Equestrian Games in Denmark, where she was ranked 4th in the world and in the Bronze Medal team.

More than just dressage, Sue-Ellen is also a long-distance rider and has ridden over 16,000 kilometres, raising $3.2 million for numerous charities, including an epic trip 2400-kilometre trip from Cairns to the Gold Coast in 1988; a total of 55 days in the saddle!

Johno and the Blind Chick is her first book. She's already hard at work on the follow-up (*Johno and the Blind Chick, Part 2*) as well as an autobiography from her own point of view.

Sue-Ellen lives in rural New South Wales with her husband Matthew, a cat called Thunder Paws and Johno.

Stay up-to-date with Sue-Ellen's adventures
on her Facebook page. Follow her at:
www.facebook.com/JohnoAndTheBlindChick/